My Little Book of Cars

Michael Worek

FIREFLY BOOKS

cars come in
different colors
and shapes

these are red,
and look fast

these cars are blue,
and also look fast

cars can go over rocks (sometimes)

but mainly drive on roads

this car is made to go over rough ground

13

electric cars are
becoming more popular

some cars are small

some cars are old

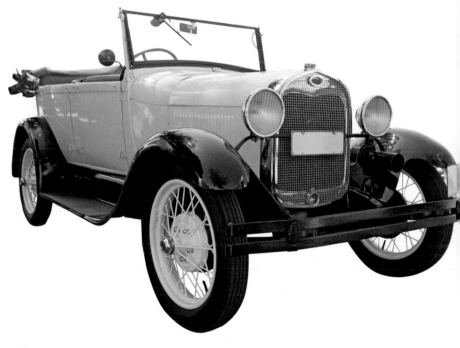

race cars can
go very fast

these small cars have lots of room inside

school bus

police car

red van

red firetruck

big trucks carry
heavy loads

this monster truck
has huge wheels

new van

old truck

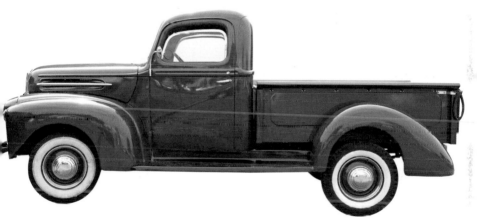

ambulance

moving van

trucks for heavy work

power shovel

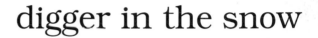

digger in the snow

yellow car

sports car

minivan

sport utility vehicles

red car

yellow car

blue car

big bus

crossing
signs

59

61

yellow car

yellow truck

motorcycles with sidecars for passengers

sport motorcycles

beautiful, shiny new cars

sports cars

orange sports car

yellow sports car

old toy car

old car

delivery vans

country highway

city highway

white SUVs

danger!

lots of room in the trunk

seat belt

buckle-up for safety

muscle car

small car

blue cars

SCHOOL BUS
EMERGENCY DOOR

STOP WHEN RED

LIGHTS FLASH

STOP

getting onto the bus

old delivery vans
— red and blue

orange car

orange pickup truck

paper map

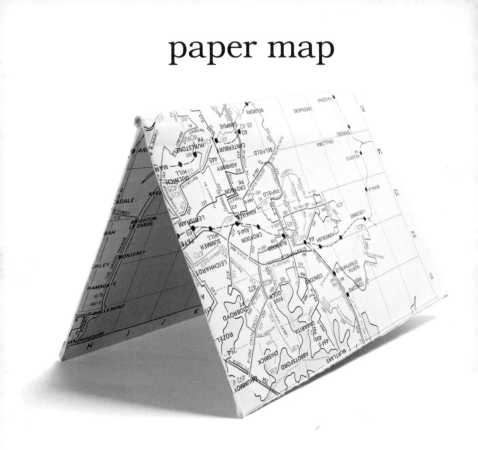

computer map

old green car

funny car

go-karts

crosswalk lights

sport utility vehicles

can you see
the difference?

crosswalk

119

ducks cross here

people cross
here

stop right here!

old cars from long ago

125

orange cars

old tires

new tire

special wheels

chains help
heavy truck
tires go in
deep snow

you can carry lots of things on the roof rack!

yellow bus

garbage truck

traffic jam —
too many cars!

tail pipes

very hot air
comes out here

tractor on the farm

engine —
makes the
car go

old red cars

big buses

149

red sports car

orange sports car

speedometer tells you how fast the car is going

02 013

1 3 2

0   20   40   60   80   100   120   140   160   180

km/h

how much gas is left in the tank?

gear
shift

foot pedals

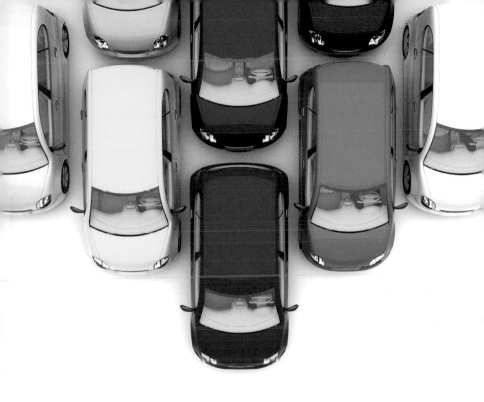

Photo Credits

A FIREFLY BOOK

Published by Firefly Books Ltd. 2013

First printing

Publisher Cataloging-in-Publication Data (U.S.)
My little book of cars / Michael Worek.
[160] p. : col. photos. ; cm.
ISBN-13: 978-1-77085-230-3
1. Cars – Pictorial works – Juvenile literature. I. Title.
[E] dc23   PZ7.M9558   2013

Library and Archives Canada Cataloguing in Publication
My little book of cars / Michael Worek.
ISBN 978-1-77085-230-3
1. Automobiles--Juvenile literature.
TL147.M9 2013   j629.222   C2013-901239-7

Published in the United States by
Firefly Books (U.S.) Inc.
P.O. Box 1338, Ellicott Station
Buffalo, New York 14205

Published in Canada by
Firefly Books Ltd.
50 Staples Avenue, Unit 1
Richmond Hill, Ontario L4B 0A7

Printed in China

The publisher gratefully acknowledges the financial support for our publishing program by the Government of Canada through the Canada Book Fund as administered by the Department of Canadian Heritage.

secrets of

ROSPERITY

J. DONALD WALTERS

Hardbound edition, first printing 1993

Copyright 1993
J. Donald Walters

Text Illustrations: Karen White

Illustrations copyright 1993
Crystal Clarity, Publishers

ISBN 1-56589-037-X

10 9 8 7 6 5 4 3 2 1

PRINTED IN HONG KONG

Crystal ♀ *Clarity*
P U B L I S H E R S

14618 Tyler Foote Road, Nevada City, CA 95959
1 (800) 424-1055

A seed thought is offered for every day of the month. Begin a day at the appropriate date. Repeat the saying several times: first out loud, then softly, then in a whisper, and then only mentally. With each repetition, allow the words to become absorbed ever more deeply into your subconscious. Thus, gradually, you will acquire as complete an understanding as one might gain from a year's course in the subject. At this point, indeed, the truths set forth here will have become your own.

Keep the book open at the pertinent page throughout the day. Refer to it occasionally during moments of leisure. Relate the saying as often as possible to real situations in your life.

Then at night, before you go to bed, repeat the thought several times more. While falling asleep, carry the words into your subconscious, absorbing their positive influence into your whole being. Let it become thereby an integral part of your normal consciousness.

DAY ONE

the secret of

ROSPERITY

is . . . .

contentment, not a bank account.

$\mathcal{D}$AY TWO

the secret of

PROSPERITY

is . . . .

happiness, for a determination
simply to be happy attracts
prosperity. Happiness is, at the same
time, the best definition
of prosperity.

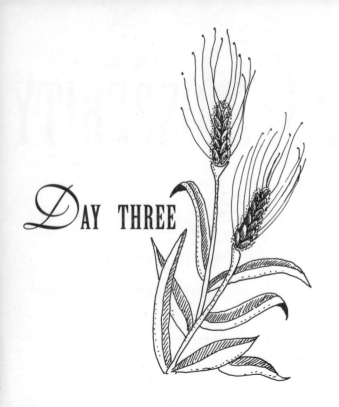

DAY THREE

the secret of

PROSPERITY

is . . . .

generosity, for by sharing with
others the good that life gives us we
open up the well-springs
of abundance.

$\mathcal{D}$AY FOUR

the secret of

PROSPERITY

is . . . .

including the good of all in your own

quest for abundance.

DAY FIVE

the secret of

PROSPERITY

Is . . . .

recognition of the part you play in
the great Symphony of Life. For Life
will sustain you, if you attune
yourself to its harmonies.

DAY SIX

the secret of

PROSPERITY

is . . . .

working with, not against, life's

changing rhythms.

DAY SEVEN

the secret of

ROSPERITY

is . . . .

looking behind the obstacles you
face in life, to the opportunities
they represent.

DAY EIGHT

the secret of

PROSPERITY

is . . . .

seeing failure as a corrective,

not as a misfortune.

DAY NINE

the secret of

PROSPERITY

is . . . .

to diversify: not your financial investments merely, as monetary counselors recommend, but—more importantly—your investments of energy. Cultivate fresh ideas, fresh interests, fresh relationships, fresh reasons for enjoying your life.

DAY TEN

the secret of

ROSPERITY

is . . . .

faith—in yourself; in others;

in Life's abundance.

DAY ELEVEN

the secret of

PROSPERITY

is . . . .

to break the hypnosis of self-limitation. The heights that any man has attained can be attained again by others—by anyone, each in his own way—given enough time, dedication, and focused energy.

DAY TWELVE

the secret of

PROSPERITY

is . . . .

not to fritter energy away with trivial
desires. A leaky faucet, drop by drop,
wastes many gallons.

$\mathscr{D}$AY THIRTEEN

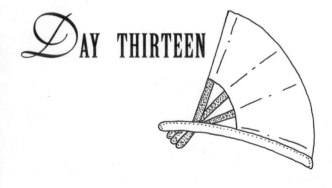

the secret of

ROSPERITY

is . . . .

finding pleasure in simplicity.

DAY FOURTEEN

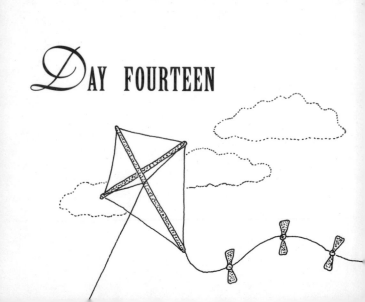

the secret of

PROSPERITY

is . . . .

holding positive expectations,

supported by a dynamic will.

DAY FIFTEEN

the secret of

PROSPERITY

is . . . .

recognizing that people can be your

best investment. Be a true

friend to all.

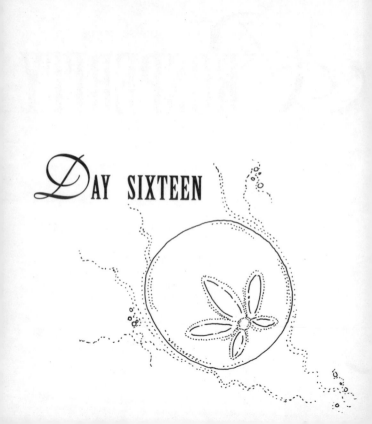

DAY SIXTEEN

the secret of

PROSPERITY

is . . . .

realizing that what you own is held by you in trust. Treat it responsibly. If you squander it, the trust will pass to another.

DAY SEVENTEEN

the secret of

PROSPERITY

is . . . .

finding strength in yourself. Don't
wait for passing waves to propel
you forward.

DAY EIGHTEEN

the secret of

PROSPERITY

is . . . .

realizing that one cannot truly prosper by the diminishment of others. Bless everyone. An expansion of self-identity is a mark of prosperity, and also a condition for its attainment.

DAY NINETEEN

the secret of

PROSPERITY

is . . . .

extending a willing hand to the
needy; helping them, above all, to
help themselves.

DAY TWENTY

the secret of

PROSPERITY

is . . . .

common sense: Don't depend on luck, but on a realistic assessment of whatever situation you face. Only in practical stages can you transform "improbables" into realities.

DAY TWENTY-ONE

the secret of

PROSPERITY

is . . . .

to remember: The higher the
mountain, the harder the effort
needed to conquer it. Success is not
for the weak-hearted. It is for those
who never rest until they attain
their ideals.

DAY TWENTY-TWO

the secret of **PROSPERITY** is . . . .

the willingness to sacrifice

non-essentials for essentials.

Day Twenty-Three

the secret of

PROSPERITY

is . . . .

to live in the present: not in past

attainments, nor in future victories.

DAY TWENTY-FOUR

the secret of

PROSPERITY

is . . . .

the patience to adjust action to
reality. In every setback, try to
understand what life is trying
to teach you.

DAY TWENTY-FIVE

the secret of

PROSPERITY

is . . . .

envying no one. View others'
successes and failures
empathetically, as your own.

DAY TWENTY-SIX

the secret of

PROSPERITY

is . . . .

inventiveness; success in any field
demands the creative outlook
of an artist.

DAY TWENTY-SEVEN

the secret of

PROSPERITY

is . . . .

to feed it daily with fresh, new
ideas—lest, like a still pond,
it stagnate.

DAY TWENTY-EIGHT

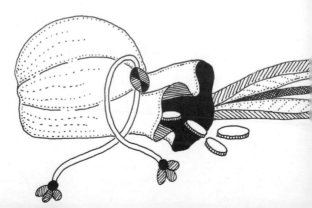

the secret of

PROSPERITY

is . . . .

to use it for the good of all, and not

to hoard it selfishly,

lest you stagnate.

DAY TWENTY-NINE

the secret of

PROSPERITY

is . . . .

a sense of proportion. Beware of

obsessions: They are an

ever-narrowing pathway.

DAY THIRTY

the secret of

PROSPERITY

is . . . .

to make time for singing. What, after
all, is prosperity, if in striving for it
one lose his capacity for song
and laughter?

DAY THIRTY-ONE

the secret of

PROSPERITY

is . . . .

remembering that the less
importance you claim for yourself,
the more importance you will
acquire in the eyes of others. Their
friendship will become, in time,
your greatest asset.

Other Books in the **Secrets** Series
by J. Donald Walters

Selected Other Titles
by J. Donald Walters

The Art of Supportive Leadership
   (book, audio, video)

How to Spiritualize Your Marriage

Education for Life

Money Magnetism

The Path (the autobiography of J. Donald Walters)

If you cannot find these books at your local gift or
bookstore, or would like our catalog, write: Crystal
Clarity, Publishers, 14618 Tyler Foote Road, Nevada
City, CA 95959, or call 1-800-424-1055.

Design: Sara Cryer
Illustrations: Karen White
Typesetting: Robert Froelick
Photography: Frank Pedrick